ARMOR &

ANIMALS

Liz Yohlin Baill

Princeton Architectural Press · New York

Philadelphia Museum of Art

What do slimy snails and shining armor have in common?

How are lobsters and knights alike?

From porcupines to people, many creatures use armor for protection.

A group of rhinos is called a crash, so stay out of the way! Like a **knight** suited up in steel, a **rhino's** heavy hide protects its big, bulky body.

Rhinos

weigh thousands of pounds,
but they run fast and reach
their top speed in no time.

Find the folds around these rhinos'
joints, which help them move in their thick,
protective skin.

Armor

was often made of metal pieces called plates that protected different parts of a person's body.

It looks heavy, but armor was light enough for knights to run, jump, and ride horses.

HEADS UP

A knight can lift
the visor to look out
of a helmet, just
like a turtle peeks out
from its shell.
What might each
of them see?

A turtle's

rounded shell is attached to its body and made of more than fifty bones. A box turtle like this one can pop its head out but pull right back inside when it wants to hide.

Helmets

also have a curvy shape to fit a person's head and protect the twenty-nine bones inside. This one was made for a kid! It fit a five-year-old to wear for sporting games called tourneys. Imagine how it would feel on your head.

SCALES,
MEET MAIL

Tiny, shiny circles make up the flexible armor on a scaly fish and a knight's shirt of mail.

**Most fish are covered
in hundreds of
scales
that bend and slide over each other.**

Scales get larger as the fish grows.
Like a tree trunk, you can learn a fish's age by
counting the growth rings on its scales.

This steel shirt is made of thousands of
        linked rings that move together to form
a chain-like fabric called

mail.

These rings also tell a story—each is stamped
with the name of an important person.

BAND

TOGETHER

How many stripes
or bands of armor
can you count
on each animal?
Find where they
overlap for
extra protection.

Armadillo

means "little armored one" in Spanish. Its back is covered with bony bands that are tough like fingernails. This one is a nine-banded armadillo.

Horses aren't born with armor, so knights gave them their own shining suits. The metal bands on the neck of this

horse armor

are connected by small nails called rivets and leather straps on the inside.

LATER
GATOR

Alligator,
meet dragon.
One is real and one
is imaginary, but
what do they have
in common?

For millions of years,

alligators

have crawled the earth.

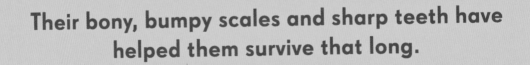

Their bony, bumpy scales and sharp teeth have
helped them survive that long.

Legends of daring

dragons

have been told for
thousands of years.

The dragon on
this piece of armor made
the horse who wore it look extra tough.
Check out its golden wings and imagine
this fire-breathing foe flying toward you.

SP⬤T ⬤N

Dots and circles
decorate the
ladybug's shell and
this shield. Both
protect something
important.

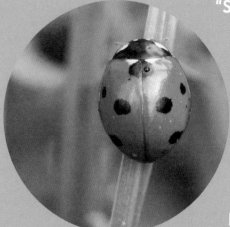

"Stop! Don't eat me!"
Like a stop sign, a

ladybug's

bright color is a warning
to other creatures.
Its wings are folded beneath
two polka-dotted shells
that move aside when the
bug is ready for takeoff.

Lots of armor is
shiny silver, but this

shield

is painted red.
A person hid behind
it for protection, like
a ladybug tucking its
wings under its own
red shields.

Ouch!
Sharp spikes
and prickly
points warn us
to stay away.

A **porcupine** rattles its quills when danger is near and can use them like tiny swords to poke predators.

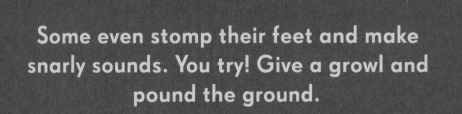

Some even stomp their feet and make snarly sounds. You try! Give a growl and pound the ground.

Guards held tall,
pointy

pole arms

while defending
princes, princesses,
and their castles.

Strike your most powerful
and protective pose,
and imagine guarding something
important to you.

LOBSTER TALES

Lots of little
pieces of shell or
steel make up these
two fierce fellows.
How else
are they alike?

The shell of a

lobster's

tail is made of six parts that
are very loosely attached
to its body. This lets the
lobster scoot backward and
wiggle away from danger.

Small metal strips
called

lames

make the legs of this
armor extra fancy
and flexible.
They look almost
like two giant
lobster tails.

Knights in full armor wore about fifty pounds of steel. Sound heavy? A snail can carry ten times its body weight on its back!

Snails

can't move very quickly,
so they need to be great at hiding.

The patterns on its swirly shell help
this sneaky snail camouflage, or blend,
with its surroundings.

Armor is not so great for hiding. It can be quite noisy and often shines in the sun.

The fancy designs on this **helmet** were meant to be admired, not for camouflage.

Kids protect their bodies too!

What do you wear as armor?

Works Illustrated

Horse Armor of Duke Ulrich of Württemberg,
Made by Wilhelm von Worms the Elder,
German, 1507; iron alloy (steel), etched and
partially gilded and blued; copper alloy (brass);
leather; textiles; weight (with saddle): 89 lb.
(40.37 kg); Gift of Athena and Nicholas Karabots
and The Karabots Foundation, 2009-117-1a–h

Field Armor, German, ca. 1500–1510; iron alloy
(steel), partially etched and engraved; copper
alloy (brass); leather; height: 70½ in. (179 cm),
weight: 61 lb. 6 oz. (27.85 kg); Bequest of Carl
Otto Kretzschmar von Kienbusch, 1977-167-4a–r

*Close Helmet for a Boy of about Five, for Use
in the Tourney,* German or Austrian, ca. 1505;
iron alloy (steel); height: 8 ¹¹⁄₁₆ in. (22 cm),
weight: 4 lb. 5 oz. (1.95 kg); Bequest of Carl
Otto Kretzschmar von Kienbusch, 1977-167-81

Hauberk (Shirt) of Mail, Persian, ca. 1600;
steel and brass, stamped with the names
of leading Shi'a imams; Bequest of Carl Otto
Kretzschmar von Kienbusch, 1977-167-259

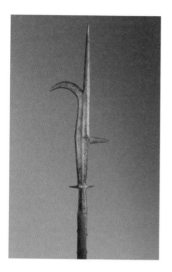

Staff Weapon (Bill, or Ronca/Roncone), Italian, ca. 1510; iron alloy (steel), partially etched and gilded; wood (replaced); height: 96 1/16 in. (267.1 cm), weight: 5 lb. 10 oz. (2565 g); Purchased with Museum funds from the Edmond Foulc Collection, 1930-1-161

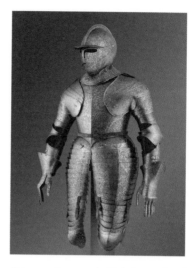

Cuirassier Armor, probably Italian or French, 1612; iron alloy (steel), etched and partially blackened; leather; height: 40 11/16 in. (103.4 cm), weight: 63 lb. (28.58 kg); Bequest of Carl Otto Kretzschmar von Kienbusch, 1977-167-36

Painted Rawhide Shield, Indian, 18th–19th century; rawhide; paint; diameter: 15 3/8 in. (39 cm); Gift of the Philadelphia Commercial Museum (also known as the Philadelphia Civic Center Museum), 2004-111-709

Helmet (Morion), Italian or French, ca. 1575–1600; etched and partially gilded steel; brass; leather; canvas; height: 16 1/4 in. (41.3 cm), weight: 4.3 lb. (19.31 kg); Bequest of Carl Otto Kretzschmar von Kienbusch, 1977-167-127

About the Philadelphia Museum of Art

The Philadelphia Museum of Art's celebrated collection invites visitors to see the world—and themselves—anew through the expressive power of the arts. Our museum is a place for visitors to spend quality creative time together, with art as a catalyst for conversation and self-reflection.

Highlights include extensive collections of South Asian and East Asian art, including our Japanese Tea House; the world's largest collection of works by Marcel Duchamp; renowned Impressionist and Post-Impressionist paintings; exceptional American painting, sculpture, furniture, silver, and ceramics; and a global contemporary art collection. Our arms and armor collection is the second largest in the United States and a perennial favorite among visitors of all ages.

Author's Note

When I was hired by the Philadelphia Museum of Art to lead weekly "Days of Knights" tours for families, I immediately discovered that armor is a favorite among kids. In these galleries, little eyes grow wider and questions come quickly. As an art educator and pacifist with a penchant for rainbows and colorful contemporary works of art, I didn't initially connect with suits of steel once used on the battlefield. The more time I spent in the armor galleries, the more enchanting I found this clothing made of metal that was somehow designed for running, jumping, and horseback riding. When I learned that my colleagues routinely compared armor to lobsters' tails, firefighters' equipment, and football gear, my curiosity was sparked and I wanted to know more.

As educators, we look for entry points to help children connect with new ideas through something familiar. *Armor & Animals* bridges kids' natural fascination with animals and the historical design feat that is armor. We hope this book ignites a sense of wonder in both children and grown-ups and inspires new ways of thinking about art and the world around us.

Armor & Animals is the product of many creative minds. For reviving and reimagining the children's publication program at the Philadelphia Museum of Art, I am deeply grateful to Katie Reilly, the William T. Ranney Director of Publishing, as well as to David Updike for his patient partnership and editorial expertise and to Mary Cason for her proofreading skills. My sincere thanks to Marla Shoemaker and Emily Schreiner for their mentorship and advocacy, and to Katy Friedland, coauthor with Marla of the museum's first children's books, for paving this path in many ways. To our partners at Princeton Architectural Press, and especially Lynn Grady, Rob Shaeffer, Sara Stemen, Paul Wagner, Natalie Snodgrass, and Lia Hunt, thank you for bringing our work to life. For their help creating the gallery activity that inspired this book, thanks to Rebecca Quinn, Amy Hewitt, and Jamie Montgomery, as well as to Luis Bravo and Nick Massarelli for developing our kiosk into a book concept. For their assistance with fact-checking, I am grateful to Virginia Friedman; Joyce and Arleen Dascola; the Philadelphia Insectarium and Butterfly Pavilion; the Adventure Aquarium, Camden, New Jersey; the Philadelphia Zoo; and the museum's J. J. Medveckis Associate Curator of Arms and Armor, Dirk Breiding. I received support from many colleagues in the Division of Education and Public Programs and offer special thanks to Caitlin Deutsch and Leigh Dale. Finally, my unending gratitude to Pam and Joe Yohlin for filling our home with art and love, and to two very special readers, Logan and Luca, and my partner and sounding board in all things, Andrew.

Liz Yohlin Baill
COLLECTIONS INTERPRETER FOR YOUTH AND FAMILIES

PUBLISHED BY
Princeton Architectural Press
202 Warren Street
Hudson, New York 12534
www.papress.com

WITH

Philadelphia Museum of Art
2525 Pennsylvania Avenue
Philadelphia, PA 19130-2440
www.philamuseum.org

ISBN 978-1-61689-955-4
Library of Congress Control Number: 2020934893

This publication was made possible by a grant
from The Women's Committee of the Philadelphia
Museum of Art.

FOR PRINCETON ARCHITECTURAL PRESS:
Editors: Rob Shaeffer and Sara Stemen
Designers: Paul Wagner and Natalie Snodgrass

FOR THE PHILADELPHIA MUSEUM OF ART:
The William T. Ranney Director of Publishing:
   Katie Reilly
Editors: David Updike with Mary Cason
Design Concept: Nick Massarelli

PHOTOGRAPHY CREDITS:
Armor photographs throughout by Graydon Wood,
Philadelphia Museum of Art Photography Studio
—
Front endpaper (right): Elen11 / iStock
Page 6 (rhino): Vladimir Wrangel / Shutterstock
Page 9 (turtle): Coahuilan Box Turtle (Terrapene
   Coahuila), amwu / iStock
Page 12 (fish): © Siarhei Nosyreu
Page 15 (armadillo): lalito / Shutterstock
Page 18 (alligator): Norbert Nagel / Wikimedia
   Commons, License: CC BY-SA 3.0
Page 20 (ladybug in flight): erhandayi
Page 21 (ladybug on grass): Tividan / Shutterstock
Page 24 (porcupine): iStock / GlobalP
Page 27 (lobster): kunst-mp / iStock
Page 30 (snail): filipfoto / iStock
Page 33 (bike helmet): John Kasawa / Shutterstock;
   (umbrella): Tatiana Popova / Shutterstock;
   (football helmet): LunaseeStudios / Shutterstock;
   (all other images): Shutterstock
Page 37 (top and left): Philadelphia Museum of Art
   Photography Studio; (right): Elizabeth Leitzell
Back endpaper (left): zazamaza / iStock